SANTA FE

IMPRESSIONS

PHOTOGRAPHY BY **LAURENCE PARENT**

TEXT BY **EMILY DRABANSKI**

FARCOUNTRY
PRESS

ISBN 10: 1-56037-451-9
ISBN 13: 978-1-56037-451-0
© 2007 by Farcountry Press
Photography © 2007 by Laurence Parent

For more information about our books, write Farcountry Press, P.O. Box 5630, Helena, MT 59604; call (800) 821-3874; or visit www.farcountrypress.com.

Created, produced, and designed in the United States. Printed in China.

12 11 10 09 08 07   1 2 3 4 5 6

Front cover: The Inn and Spa at Loretto has a festive air both inside and out during the holiday season. In addition to hotel rooms, there are boutiques and galleries on the premises. Also, an interior hallway leads to the adjacent Loretto Chapel.

Back cover: Chimney Rock at Ghost Ranch in Abiquiú stands sentinel in this land that many call O'Keeffe Country. It's one of the more famous landmarks that artist Georgia O'Keeffe enjoyed as she walked near her Abiquiú home.

Title page: In 1937, architect John Gaw Meem designed the First Presbyterian Church, which was recently renovated to preserve the structure's integrity and better serve today's congregation.

Right: About a half hour south of Santa Fe, the frozen Cochiti Lake glistens on a winter's day while snow blankets the Ortiz Mountains in the distance.

Below: Artist Reynaldo "Sonny" Rivera and landscape architect Richard Borkovetz collaborated on this sculpture on Museum Hill titled *Journey's End,* which depicts travelers on the Santa Fe Trail.

FOREWORD

Emily Drabanski

Editor, *New Mexico Magazine*

Snow dusts the entry of Klaudia Marr Gallery, one of several galleries featuring a wide variety of art along Canyon Road, known as Artists' Road.

Turquoise skies, the scent of roasting chiles, the warmth that radiates from thick adobe walls, the twirling crimson skirts of flamenco dancers, the steady drum beats at a Pueblo dance, and spectacular sunsets that bathe the mountains in a kaleidoscope of colors—just a few Santa Fe impressions that will linger long after your visit to New Mexico's historic capital city.

Photographer Laurence Parent's skillful compositions richly capture many of these magical moments. Born north of Santa Fe in Española, Laurence has explored the city since he was a child. As an editor at *New Mexico Magazine,* I recognize the power and emotion behind his photographs. I also know that he gets a lot of great photographs that others miss because he'll do whatever it takes to create the ideal shot. He climbs to the top of a mountain to catch the perfect sunset. He endures a rainstorm to capture the dew-covered pines as a double rainbow emerges. He trudges through the snow to experience the crystalline winter glow beneath a full moon. He's done all this to preserve the enchantment of Santa Fe.

To Spanish speakers, Santa Fe means "holy faith." In 1608, Pedro de Peralta, the second provincial governor, named the city La Villa Real de Santa Fé, the Royal Town of Santa Fe. Today there remains a regal air—what some call a sacred spirit—about the city.

As the setting sun paints the mountains on the eastern horizon in rich red hues, one can see why the early Spanish explorers referred to them as the Sangre de Cristos, the "blood of Christ." Nearby Pueblo Indians, whose ancestors were here long before the Spanish explorers, also found these mountains to be a source of spiritual energy. Today, people of all faiths and cultural backgrounds still journey to this multi-cultural city perched at 7,000 feet to find inspiration.

To truly experience the City Different, as Santa Fe is called, stroll around the Santa Fe Plaza—the heart of the city. During the day, on the north side of the Plaza, under the Portal of the Palace of the Governors, American Indians from a variety of tribes spread out blankets and sell their jewelry and pottery. At night, live music brings out a diverse crowd who can just as easily scoot with their cowboy boots or kick up their high heels to some lively salsa.

This thriving plaza was once one of the busiest trading hubs in the West. Look at a Santa Fe map. The streets are not aligned in a typical grid. The city looks more like a spider web, with its meandering streets that once guided burros, horses, and wagons to the plaza. To the south, Santa Fe's Agua Fria Street was part of El Camino Real, the Royal Road that brought trade and travelers back and forth between

An article in Harper's Magazine *in 1879 first referred to this structure as the Oldest House in the United States. While it's difficult to verify the exact age of the building, it was probably built in the 1600s, when the first Spanish colonists started to settle in the area. Tree-ring dating of the vigas (log roof supports) indicates the building was contructed in 1646. The Oldest House, also known as La Casa Vieja de Analco, on DeVargas Street is a popular tourist stop. Local lore suggests that "spirits" have been seen and felt in the building, even in modern times.*

Santa Fe and Mexico. To the east, traces of the Santa Fe Trail are reminders of the hundreds of soldiers, families, and traders who made the arduous journey to the city from Independence, Missouri. Later, trains brought Easterners who were wowed by the mystique of the West. When travel by car came in vogue, the original path of the venerable U.S. Route 66 veered north to bring travelers into Santa Fe.

Artists are also drawn here, mesmerized by the clarity of light. Most notably, Georgia O'Keeffe, who lived in nearby Abiquiú, showed the world that one could create great art far away from the hustle and bustle of the East. Today, Santa Fe's museums, galleries, and world-class cultural events beckon art aficionados.

For lovers of nature, the nearby mountains offer opportunities for quiet reflection or high-altitude adventures. Cyclists love the challenge of the steep inclines of Hyde Park Road at Santa Fe Ski Basin. Hikers like to explore at a more leisurely pace, particularly during the fall, when the mountains explode with the golden hues of shimmering aspen leaves. In the winter, skiers and snowboarders experience the adrenaline rush of downhill excitement.

Santa Fe beckons you to linger, explore, and reflect. Laurence Parent's breathtaking photographs invite you to do the same.

Traditionally, people dried chile by stringing and hanging chile ristras in the fall; the chile was then ground up and used in a variety of dishes. The crimson chile ristras look so striking against adobe walls that today many people integrate them into their home décor.

After a welcome rainfall, a double rainbow stretches across the sky, creating a perfect frame for this Santa Fe Southern Railway caboose. The train carries sightseers thirty-six miles roundtrip between Santa Fe and the nearby village of Lamy. Families usually opt for the afternoon trains. Those looking for a romantic ride generally choose the sunset departures.

Left: The Nedra Matteucci Galleries showcase the work of many prominent artists and sculptors. At the front entrance to the courtyard of the gallery on Paseo de Peralta are sculptures by Dan Ostermiller. The rabbit sculpture titled *Lola* is one of an edition of twelve bronzes. The bronze buffalo, *Sovereign,* is one of an edition of nine. Priscilla Hoback's stoneware mural *The Big Dipper and the Dog Star* hangs above them.

Below: The galleries on Canyon Road bustle with openings and special events on Friday nights during the summer and fall. On this quiet, snowy winter day, the lovely, lavender trim on the door and windows of Jane Sauer's Thirteen Moons Gallery seems to invite visitors to come in out of the cold.

Right, top: The Santa Fe Children's Museum makes learning fun. This youngster enjoys the giant bubbles produced in one of the many hands-on exhibits.

Right, bottom: Leslie Miller and Liz Sobel created this colorful mural outside the Santa Fe Children's Museum. Although the scene is quiet in winter, in summer boisterous children happily explore the various outdoor exhibits.

Far right: The Bataan Memorial Military Museum is just a few doors down from the Santa Fe Children's Museum off Old Santa Fe Trail. Many New Mexicans were part of the grueling Bataan Death March during World War II. The museum showcases military memorabilia and shares the stories of the soldiers who were forced to make the journey.

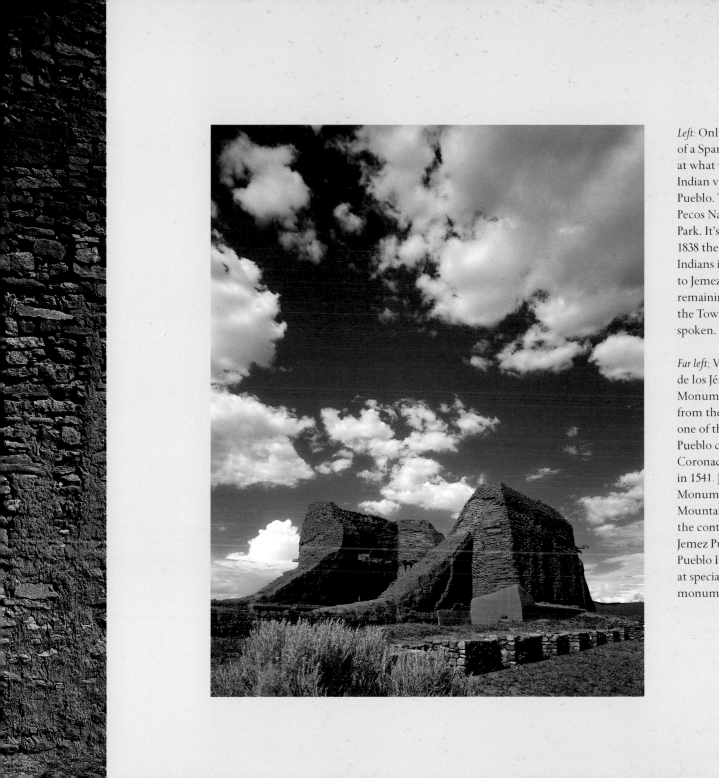

Left: Only the thick walls of a Spanish mission remain at what was once a Towa Indian village called Pecos Pueblo. The site is now Pecos National Historical Park. It's believed that in 1838 the few remaining Indians in the area moved to Jemez Pueblo, the only remaining pueblo where the Towa language is spoken.

Far left: Visitors to San José de los Jémez at Jémez State Monument can see ruins from the original site of one of the seven Jemez Pueblo communities that Coronado encountered in 1541. Jémez State Monument in the Jémez Mountains is not far from the contemporary site of Jemez Pueblo. The Jemez Pueblo Indians often dance at special events at the monument.

13

Right, top: This striking stone sculpture titled *Rising Spirit* was carved by Chippewa artist Rollie Grandbois and is one of the many larger-than-life sculptures on the grounds of the New Mexico State Capitol.

Below: Estella Loretto's sculpture *Offerings for a Good Life* welcomes visitors to the capitol, called the Roundhouse because it is shaped like the Zia sun symbol displayed prominently on New Mexico's state flag. Estella Loretto was born in nearby Jemez Pueblo and operates a gallery in Santa Fe. Visitors can tour the capitol and are encouraged to see the impressive Capitol Arts collection, which showcases work by some of the state's top artists. The Governor's Gallery on the fourth floor features changing art exhibitions.

Far right: A backpacker travels one of the many trails traversing the Pecos Wilderness in the Santa Fe National Forest near Santa Fe. Even in the summer months, the highest peaks are sometimes dusted with snow.

Left: Storm clouds pass over San José de la Gracia Church in Las Trampas on the High Road to Taos. Many visitors to Santa Fe take the National Scenic Byway known as the High Road to travel to Taos. Las Trampas was established in 1750 by twelve families who came from Santa Fe led by Juan de Arguello.

Facing page: One of the newest national monuments, Kasha-Katuwe Tent Rocks National Monument offers hikers a chance to see these otherworldly geological wonders. The monument is operated with respect for members of nearby Cochiti Pueblo, and road access occasionally is limited due to special closed ceremonies at the pueblo.

Right: Streetlights create a pattern of light and shadow in the portal of the Institute of American Indian Arts Museum in downtown Santa Fe. The Institute of American Indian Art's main campus is located on the south side of Santa Fe; its students are affiliated with tribes from throughout the United States and Canada. The institute's strong arts program and talented faculty also attract non-Indians, who study a variety of subjects, including jewelry making, sculpture, painting, photography, and creative writing.

Facing page: The Santa Fe Plaza is truly the heart of Santa Fe. Although quiet on this winter's night, during the summer it fills with people relaxing on benches and milling about. For centuries the plaza has been the focal point for Santa Fe events. It is the staging ground for the Spanish Market in July, the Santa Fe Indian Market in August, and Fiesta de Santa Fe in September.

Right: A series of steps take visitors from street level on Paseo de Peralta to Santa Fe's Cross of the Martyrs. The city's Fiesta de Santa Fe, a week-long celebration in September, closes with a solemn candlelight procession from the St. Francis Cathedral to the Cross of the Martyrs.

Below: La Fonda, which means "hotel" in Spanish, was often a final stop on the Santa Fe Trail. This overhead shot of the main restaurant from the mezzanine shows some of the Old World charm that pervades this hotel on the Santa Fe Plaza.

Left: The Miraculous Staircase in the Loretto Chapel has drawn visitors from around the world, who marvel at the artistry of the wooden staircase. After the chapel was built, the Sisters of Loretto had no easy way to access the choir loft; so they prayed a novena to St. Joseph, the patron saint of carpenters. According to local lore, a mysterious carpenter (thought to be St. Joseph) appeared, built the staircase, and then vanished. Research in recent years has revealed that the carpenter might have been François-Jean "Frenchy" Rochas, a master French woodworker. Regardless of the carpenter's true identity, the sisters' prayers were answered with one of the most beautiful staircases in the country.

Far left: At sunset, electric *farolitos,* or "little lanterns," glow along rooftops at the Inn and Spa at Loretto. The structure's architecture echoes the forms of ancient adobe Pueblo buildings, particularly the multi-storied buildings seen in Taos Pueblo. Many Santa Feans still put out the traditional lit candles in paper bags on Christmas Eve.

23

Right, top: Established in 1610, the Palace of the Governors was New Mexico's first capitol. Believed to be the oldest continually occupied public building in the United States, the Palace of the Governors is now a museum that chronicles the history of Santa Fe and New Mexico. In addition to permanent displays and changing exhibitions, the museum hosts many special events that fill the interior courtyard throughout the year, including Christmas at the Palace and the annual Mountain Man Rendezvous.

Right, bottom: Visitors enjoy interacting with Indian vendors who sell their work under the Portal of the Palace of the Governors. All vendors are carefully screened to ensure the work is authentic and made by the Indians who sell it.

Facing page: El Zaguan on Canyon Road houses the Historic Santa Fe Foundation offices. In Spanish, *el zaguan* refers to a building's breezeway, depicted in this photograph. The Historic Santa Fe Foundation works to preserve the architectural integrity of downtown Santa Fe.

L ÉTAIT UNE FOIS un
gentilhomme qui épousa,
en secondes noces, une
femme, la plus hautaine & la plus
fière qu'on
avait deux
qui lui re
choses.
une jeune
& d'une b
tenait cela
meilleure
sa mauvaise humeur : elle ne put
souffrir les bonnes qualités de cette
jeune enfant, qui rendaient ses
filles encore plus haïssables. Elle la
chargea des plus viles occupations
de la maison
nettoyait la vaisselle &
qui frottait la chambre
& celles de mesdem
elle couchait to
maison,
avaient des
& des miroi
depuis les p
pauvre fill
patience &
son père, qu
Cendrillon
redeviendrait citrouille
souris
carrosse
ses chevaux

Left: A production of Cinderella entertains patrons of the world-renowned Santa Fe Opera. The summer season features classic operas, as well as world premieres of innovative productions.
PHOTO COURTESY OF THE SANTA FE OPERA

Below: The Santa Fe Opera's renovations have enhanced the elegant outdoor venue, providing a sweeping roof overhead to protect against the elements and open sides to allow in the balmy summer night air. Elegant tailgate parties in the parking lot at sunset are a long tradition, particularly on opening night.
PHOTO BY ROBERT RECK, COURTESY OF THE SANTA FE OPERA

Left: As you take a summer stroll along Canyon Road, steal away to one of the many courtyards and enjoy a respite among the beautiful gardens. During summer and fall, many of the galleries stay open later on Friday nights for special exhibition openings and gallery receptions.

Below: The Lensic Performing Arts Center, a renovated classic movie theater, has added new energy to downtown. It regularly offers concerts by the Santa Fe Symphony and Chorus and Pro Música, as well as brings in touring national acts such as the dance group Pilobolus and pop sensations such as the Neville Brothers. The Lannan Foundation's popular Readings and Conversations event regularly presents top authors and poets for a very reasonable price. And yes, they often feature classic movies rarely seen these days on the big screen.

Left: Located on the road to the Santa Fe ski area, Ten Thousand Waves beckons skiers, cyclists, and hikers to stop for a relaxing hot bath. The Japanese-style spa offers not only hot tubs but massage and a variety of skin care and spa treatments. With Japanese lanterns adding to the aesthetic, you'll feel as though you've been transported to the other side of the globe rather than into the mountains just minutes from downtown Santa Fe.

Below: Ten Thousand Waves' outdoor hot tubs are a favorite place for skiers to unwind on winter afternoons. Others drop by at night when the glow of moonlight illuminates the snow for evenings of true enchantment.

Right: Craig Dan Goseyun's commanding sculpture *Apache Mountain Spirit Dancer* greets visitors to the Museum of Indian Arts and Culture. Milner Plaza ties this museum to the nearby Museum of International Folk Art. In the summer, Milner Plaza often is the center for special events, such as Indian dances and the popular Santa Fe International Folk Art Market. Just a short drive away, also on Museum Hill, are two privately run museums: the Museum of Spanish Colonial Art and the Wheelwright Museum of the American Indian. Walking paths through the juniper-studded foothills surround the museums.

Below: The Museum of Fine Arts, located off the Santa Fe Plaza, houses an extensive permanent collection of Southwestern works by Georgia O'Keeffe, artists of the early New Mexico art colonies, and contemporary artists. The museum features special exhibitions ranging from contemporary works to world-class traveling art exhibitions featuring works by the masters. The popular Santa Fe Chamber Music Festival presents most of its concerts in the St. Francis Auditorium.

Above: The Loretto Chapel glows at sunset. Brides and grooms from around the world come to be married in the charming Gothic chapel featuring the famous Miraculous Staircase.

Facing page: In recent years, St. Francis Cathedral was designated as the Cathedral Basilica of St. Francis of Assisi by Pope Benedict XVI. The church, designed by a French architect and built by Italian stonemasons, took a central role in Willa Cather's novel *Death Comes to the Archbishop.* The title refers to Archbishop Jean Baptiste Lamy, who guided the construction from 1869 to 1893. The archbishop's desire for a more French-style Gothic cathedral disregarded the cultural preferences of the Hispanic people, who favored the more traditional thick-walled adobe mission churches.

Below: This more traditional adobe church, Santuario de Guadalupe, was built to honor Our Lady of Guadalupe. The church, built between 1776 and 1795, is thought to be the oldest shrine built to Our Lady of Guadalupe in the United States. El Santuario, operated by the Catholic Church, still has religious services and offers the space for a limited number of classical concerts and special lectures.

Right: The magnificent San Miguel Mission is open daily for tours and still offers Mass on Sundays. One of the oldest churches in the country, it is located in the historic Barrio de Analco area, which is believed to have been settled by Indians from Mexico in the 1200s. Note the traditional hand-hewn wooden vigas (ceiling supports).

Far right: The High Road to Taos from Santa Fe passes through several traditional Hispanic villages. In those communities, you'll find many traditional adobe churches, including El Santuario de Chimayó. Called the Lourdes of the Americas, it attracts visitors from around the world who come for what some believe is "miraculous dirt" that has the power to heal ailments—both physical and emotional. The room is filled with crutches, notes, and other mementos from those who've made the pilgrimage. On Good Friday, thousands of pilgrims make a religious pilgrimage to El Santuario de Chimayó. Some walk for days from throughout the state.

Above: The Great Seal of the State of New Mexico declares the year of statehood, 1912. Although New Mexico was one of the first areas settled by Europeans in the Americas, it was the forty-seventh state admitted into the Union.

Left: Known for its array of traditional New Mexican dishes and continental cuisine, the Pink Adobe Restaurant, known locally as The Pink, is a favorite with Santa Feans and tourists alike. The late proprietor, Rosalea Murphy, was a colorful Santa Fe character who opened the restaurant in 1944 in the 300-year-old house and developed many of her own specialties, including the popular gypsy stew. When ordering New Mexican food, you'll be asked the official state question: red or green? (in reference to the two types of chile). Can't make up your mind? Do what the locals do and respond, "Christmas," to get a little of both.

Left: For a day trip into northern New Mexico, head up to Carson National Forest in the San Juan Mountains near Chama.

Facing page: El Rancho de los Golondrinas, a living history museum, is located south of Santa Fe in La Cienega at one of the original stops on El Camino Royal (the Royal Road from Mexico). On summer and fall weekends, a variety of events take place, including Civil War re-enactments, wine festivals, and a traditional harvest festival complete with demonstrations of traditional crafts such as tinworking and Río Grande-style weaving.

41

Right, top: Ski Santa Fe offers a variety of runs for both beginning and expert skiers. The ski area also welcomes snowboarders.

Right, bottom: Skiers enjoy the spectacular vistas and the exhilarating fresh air atop the runs at Ski Santa Fe.

Far right: Snow-capped pines take on a rose-colored glow at sunset atop the Sangre de Cristo Mountains in Santa Fe National Forest. The Spanish named the mountains Sangre de Cristo, meaning the "blood of Christ," in reference to shades of red seen on the mountains at sunset.

Left: Breathtaking vistas, such as this view of the lush Chama Valley and the red rock cliffs of Ghost Ranch, inspired artist Georgia O'Keeffe.

Below: El Rancho de las Golondrinas de La Conquistadora chapel at El Rancho de las Golondrinas is built in the style of a traditional morada, a windowless adobe church used by the Penitentes—a brotherhood of devout Catholic men who carry on traditional religious observances. Visitors can tour this morada, but others are open only to Hermanos, members of the brotherhood.

Above: Chile ristras, cow skulls, and clay pots from Mexico are just some of the treasures you'll find at the original Jackalope store in Santa Fe. Kids love visiting the prairie dog village, and adults enjoy exploring the various buildings filled with souvenirs and crafts from around the world. In the summer, an outdoor café offers entertainment.

Left: Hand-carved wooden corbels and carefully applied paint add to the rustic look of this *portal* in one of the courtyards off Palace Avenue.

Right: Bluffs and mesas capture the light, and the Sangre de Cristo Mountains can be seen in the distance from this scenic vista near Los Alamos and Bandelier National Monument.

Below: Petroglyph National Monument near Albuquerque showcases many fine examples of petroglyphs, which were carved by ancient Indians. Petroglyphs can be seen throughout northern New Mexico, primarily along the Río Grande.

Left: Golden aspens shimmer as the sun sets on the Santa Fe National Forest.

Below: The Cathedral Basilica of St. Francis of Assisi takes on a golden hue as darkness falls on the capital city. Many consider St. Francis to be the patron saint of Santa Fe.

Right, top: Visitors can hike to Tyuoni Ruins and Talus House at Bandelier National Monument, located less than an hour from Santa Fe.

Right, bottom: This shot taken from a trail high above the Tyuoni ruins offers a view of the remnants of walls that once separated the rooms.

Facing page: A winding trail at Bandelier National Monument leads to the spectacular Upper Falls at Frijoles Creek. This popular day trip takes hikers through the scenic backcountry.

Right, top: The Invocation by Buck McCain is one of the many sculptures at the Shidoni Sculpture Garden in Tesuque. Bronze sculptures are poured at the Shidoni Foundry. An indoor gallery showcases smaller pieces and other types of art.

Right, bottom: Allan Houser's sculpture *Heading Home* stands outside the entry of the Wheelwright Museum of the American Indian. The museum was designed in the shape of a traditional Navajo structure called a hogan.

Facing page: Spend the afternoon strolling through the Shidoni Sculpture Garden in Tesuque. On Saturdays, visitors can see a bronze pouring at the foundry. Tesuque also features a glass-blowing studio, restaurant, and café. The charming village with its cottonwood-lined roads is approximately fifteen minutes north of Santa Fe.

Right: The San Miguel Mission celebrates Mass on Sundays and is open for tours during the rest of the week. One of the Christian Brothers who operates the mission is usually on hand to answer questions.

Far right: The Randall Davey Audubon Center on Upper Canyon Road offers trails for bird watching. The property includes the former home of Santa Fe-artist Randall Davey, who painted the murals both inside and outside of the building.

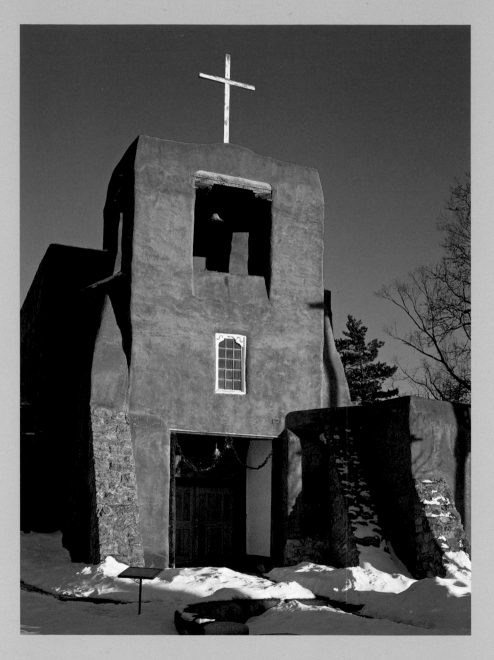

Left: Stewart Lake is one of many scenic alpine lakes visitors enjoy in the Pecos Wilderness in the Santa Fe National Forest.

Below: The sunlit Sangre de Cristo Mountains provide a lush backdrop for this rustic barn and cottonwoods in the Pojoaque Valley, approximately twenty minutes north of Santa Fe.

Right: In the summer, afternoon monsoon storms bring much-needed rain. Cristo Rey Church radiates a warm glow as the sun returns and storm clouds drift toward the mountains.

Below: The peaceful Sena Plaza, located off of Palace Avenue, provides a welcome escape from the hustle and bustle of the downtown area. Shops, galleries, and La Casa Sena Restaurant surround Sena Plaza. At night, stop in La Cantina to hear waiters sing popular show tunes from Broadway musicals.

Left: In fall, drive an hour and a half north of Santa Fe and marvel at the golden aspens tucked in Santa Barbara Canyon. In the background, a storm brews on nearby Jicarita Peak, a mountain sacred to the Picuris Pueblo Indians.

Below: Stately cottonwoods drape golden leaves along the Chama River Valley. The red and pink striated rock cliffs tower in the background.

Right: Wildflowers bloom around Serpent Lake in the Sangre de Cristo Mountains.

Below: The rugged Truchas Peaks cast a shadow on Upper Trampas Lake. *Truchas* is Spanish for "trout."

Left: The Museum of Fine Arts was founded in 1917. The Pueblo Revival building was designed by I. H. and William M. Rapp. The building's architectural style incorporates influences from the Spanish missions found in the pueblos. It's generally thought that the museum's architecture inaugurated what people now call Santa Fe Style.

Below: When the First Presbyterian Church of Santa Fe was established in 1867, it was the only Protestant church in the Territory of New Mexico.

Above: Hikers take in a scenic vista along a trail at the Kasha Katuwe Tent Rocks National Monument near Cochiti, south of Santa Fe.

Left: A misty morning in Valle Grande in the Valles Caldera National Preserve. The preserve's peaceful setting belies the fact that the area was shaped by violent volcanic eruptions. The 89,000 acres were a private ranch until 2000, when Congress created the preserve. The number of visitors is restricted through a reservation system. Visitors can hunt, cross-country ski, go on van tours, or hike. Two of the most popular activities are sleigh and wagon rides.

Take a day trip to northern New Mexico where you can catch the sunset, which casts a rosy glow over the Sangre de Cristo Mountains.

Left, top: The Joe Wade Fine Arts gallery showcases art that reflects the spirit of the Southwest.

Left, bottom: Many murals grace walls throughout Santa Fe, such as this one in the Guadalupe Street area.

Facing page: When the Georgia O'Keeffe Museum opened in July 1997, it was the first museum in the United States dedicated to a single woman artist. The museum showcases a variety of O'Keeffe's work, including her well-known large-scale flowers and depictions of the deserts and desert cliffs she so loved in the Abiquiú area. The Georgia O'Keeffe Museum is the largest single repository of her work in the world. The museum also exhibits a variety of her American modernist contemporaries, such as Andy Warhol and Jackson Pollock.

Right: The setting sun casts long shadows across the ruins of the Spanish mission at Pecos National Historical Park. It's near the village of Pecos, which beckons you to explore the surrounding mountains, as well as fish in the Pecos River.

Below: The large hand-carved double doors invite you to enter the Arnold and Doris Roland Sculpture Garden at the Museum of Indian Arts and Culture.

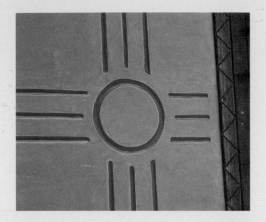

Above: The Zia sun symbol, which is featured on the New Mexico state flag, is etched into a building on San Francisco Street.

Right: An array of adobes form the arched entryway on Acequia Madre. *Acequia* is the Spanish term for "irrigation ditch." Every spring those living along the *acequias* throughout northern New Mexico participate in an annual clean-up.

Far right: A thick-walled adobe entryway welcomes visitors as they enter the Nedra Matteucci Galleries on Paseo de Peralta. The gallery features paintings by the old Santa Fe and Taos masters, as well as contemporary Southwestern paintings, sculpture, and jewelry. In the back of the gallery, many sculptures are displayed in the expansive, verdant courtyard.

Homes dot the foothills at the base of the Sangre de Cristo Mountains where a rainstorm brews. In the arid Southwest, folks pray for rain to nurture the land.

Laurence Parent

Laurence Parent was born and raised in New Mexico. After receiving a petroleum engineering degree at the University of Texas at Austin in 1981, he practiced engineering for six years before becoming a full-time freelance photographer and writer specializing in landscape, travel, and nature subjects. His photos appear in numerous calendars. His many article and photo credits include *National Geographic Traveler*, *Men's Journal*, *Outside*, *Backpacker*, *Sierra*, *Natural History*, *National Parks*, *Newsweek*, *Arizona Highways*, *Travel & Leisure*, and the *New York Times*. Laurence contributes regularly to regional publications such as *Texas Highways*, *Texas Monthly*, *New Mexico Magazine*, and *Texas Parks & Wildlife*. Laurence has had more than thirty books published.

He makes his home in the Austin area with his wife Patricia and two children.